WITHDRAWN

HAGAR'S
DAUGHTERS

The Madeleva Lecture series annually commemorates the opening of the Center for Spirituality of Saint Mary's College, Notre Dame, Indiana, and honors the memory of the woman who inaugurated the college's pioneering program in theology, Sister Madeleva, C.S.C.

HAGAR'S DAUGHTERS

Womanist Ways of Being in the World

DIANA L. HAYES

1995 Madeleva Lecture
in Spirituality

PAULIST PRESS
New York/Mahwah

Acknowledgments
The poem "Women" is taken from *Revolutionary Petunias & Other Poems*, copyright © 1970 by Alice Walker and reprinted by permission of Harcourt Brace & Company. Excerpts from "In Search of Our Mothers' Gardens" and "Gifts of Power: The Writings of Rebecca Jackson" are taken from the book *In Search of Our Mothers' Gardens: Womanist Prose*, copyright © 1981 by Alice Walker and reprinted by permission of Harcourt Brace & Company. The poem "The Chain" by Christine Craig is reprinted from her book *Quadrille for Tigers* published by Mina Press, Sebastapol, CA. Permission to reprint selections from *Beloved* © 1987 by Toni Morrison was granted by International Creative Management, Inc. The excerpt from the poem "I Am a Black Woman," © 1970 by Mari Evans, is reprinted by permission of the author.

Library of Congress Cataloging-in-Publication Data

Hayes, Diana L.
    Hagar's daughters : womanist ways of being in the world / Diana L. Hayes.
        p.   cm. — (Madeleva lecture in spirituality : 1995)
    Includes bibliographical references.
    ISBN 0-8091-3563-9
    1. Womanist theology. 2. Afro-American women—Religious life. I. Title. II. Series
BT83.9.H38 1995   94-48757
230'.082—dc20   CIP

Published by Paulist Press
997 Macarthur Boulevard
Mahwah, NJ 07430

Printed and bound in the
United States of America

Diana L. Hayes earned a B.A. degree from the State University of New York at Buffalo and a J.D. degree from the National Law Center at George Washington University. For a time she practiced law in New York, then studied theology at the Catholic University of America and the Catholic University of Louvain in Belgium where she received a Ph.D. in religious studies and was the first African-American woman to earn an S.T.D. (Doctor of Sacred Theology). She is presently a tenured associate professor of theology at Georgetown University and serves as an adjunct faculty member for the Master of Theology in Black Catholic Studies program at Xavier University, New Orleans. Dr. Hayes is the author of three books to be published in 1995. In addition to this Madeleva Lecture, she will publish *Trouble Don't Last Always: Soul Prayers*. Her book *And Still We Rise: An Introduction to Black Liberation Theology* is forthcoming from Paulist Press.

HAGAR'S DAUGHTERS: WOMANIST WAYS OF BEING IN THE WORLD

> I
> am a black woman
> tall as a cypress
> strong
> beyond all definition still
> defying place
> and time
> and circumstance
>   assailed
>   impervious
>   indestructible
> Look
> on me and be
>   renewed
>
> *Mari Evans*[1]

These powerfully evocative words of poet Mari Evans proclaim the vision of Black women which has extended over time and place, from Africa's deepest hinterlands to the varied lands and places of the African diaspora.

It is a vision that is proud yet humble, grace-

1

filled yet conscious of the many graces all too often denied that evocation of Black womanhood, especially in the past few hundred years.

Black women, like all women, have a history—a history that, for centuries has, in many ways, been "lost, stolen, or strayed" from the massive tomes in which the conquests and victories of people have, heretofore, been inscribed. Theirs is a history of Black women, against all odds, passing down from mother to child, the knowledge necessary to "keep on keeping on" through any and all challenges to them.

I, too, am a Black woman:

My presence in the Catholic Church...has been one of constant challenge, both for myself and (ironically) for those with whom I have come into contact. I have been challenged, in many ways, to prove not only my existence, but the validity of my existence in the face of so many others who are not like me at all. For as a Black, Catholic theologian who is very much a woman, I am, in many ways, doubly if not triply oppressed (by reason of race, class, and gender). It has been a constant struggle, therefore, for me to define not only who but whose I was. That struggle has included finding, acknowledging, and eventually rejoicing in my very own voice, a voice unlike anyone else's because it arises out of the very depths of my being, of who I am as a Black, a Catholic, and a woman.[2]

Thus, it is of critical importance to me that you recognize that what I say to you today arises from a particular context, my own as a Black, Catholic, female theologian and my sisters, other Black women of the diaspora, of different faiths, coming from different academic and professional backgrounds, but connected by what we share—the challenge of being Black and female in the United States, both today and throughout our history in this land. I have attempted, therefore, to use their stories, their histories, and their voices in the preparation of this paper and have chosen to write and present it in a style and manner which, hopefully, is reflective of their experience and speaks to them at whatever status they may have attained, Ph.D., J.D. or no D! It is important to me that my voice, which has been shaped by my own unique experience of being a daughter and granddaughter of proud and strong Black women who did not allow the limitations of their circumstances to shape their or their children's perspective on life, be presented in the context of our shared Blackness; a Blackness that emerges from the history of our people's enslavement, the experience of discrimination, Jim Crow laws and their attendant abuses, yet an experience in which we have managed, through and despite it all, to pass on our hopes, dreams, and aspirations to our children, whether born from our loins or not.

It is necessary, as Patricia Hill Collins notes, for us to explicitly ground our, that is, Black women's, analysis in multiple voices in order to highlight the diversity, richness, and power of Black women's ideas as part of a long-standing African-American women's intellectual community. This approach, she notes, counteracts the tendency of mainstream scholarship to canonize a few Black women as spokespersons for the group and then refuse to listen to any but those select few.[3]

Collins depicts Black women as "outsiders-within" because of their status as domestics and nurturers of the children of the dominant group—an ambivalent position in many ways but one which enabled them to be privy to the lives of "white elites" in ways Black men and the elite themselves were not. This led to a different per-spective, "a distinct view of the contradictions between the dominant group's actions and ide-ologies," which enabled a "new angle of vision on the process of the suppression" of white women by their men.[4] But this was a vision which, at the same time, never enabled the Black women to truly become "sisters" to their white employers or, despite its constant assertion, "like one of the family" in any but a superficial way.

As one of those "outsiders-within" in the world of academia, I, and my Black sisters, have been marginalized, yet, at the same time, strangely empowered, given authority we have not sought to speak for all Black women and, indeed, all Blacks. Yet, we have rarely been seen as subjects of our own history, engaged willingly and willfully in explorations of our own, but rather as objects whose concerns and problems as well as their resolution are raised up, possibly, for others' exploration and resolution.

Maria W. Stewart, the first Black woman political writer in the United States, asked: "How long shall the fair daughters of Africa be compelled to bury their minds and talents beneath a load of iron pots and kettles?"[5]

Today, womanist scholars are revealing that the minds and talents of Black women were not fully engaged with those "pots and kettles," but sought consistently to express themselves in a world which did not always welcome their creativity. They responded then and now to her call, first expressed in 1831:

> O, ye daughters of Africa!
> Awake! Arise! No longer sleep nor slumber,
> but distinguish yourselves, show forth to the
> world that ye are endowed with noble and
> exalted faculties.[6]

Her daughters of today take up her boldly thrown gauntlet, holding it high, and proclaiming, in their own voices and those of their mothers and fore-mothers, those sheroes of the Black world, their experiences as Black women, both in the world and in the Christian churches, for all to witness.

We are the daughters of Maria Stewart, of Ida B. Wells Barnett, of Harriet Tubman, of Sojourner Truth, of Mary McLeod Bethune, of Rebecca Jackson, of Zora Neale Hurston, and of Hagar, the rejected and cast-out slave, mother of Ishmael, concubine of Abraham and threat to Sarah, his barren wife.

Why Hagar, you ask? Was she not merely a victim, like so many women both before and after her? Was she not simply fulfilling the role destined for her—that of "an exploited and persecuted" female slave who owned nothing, not even her self?

Yes and no. "Victimhood" today has become, ironically, almost a "red badge of courage" to be held up and flaunted and thereby relieved of all sin and wrongdoing. Was this Hagar's situation, or can it be viewed through a different lens; eyed from a new perspective?

Hagar was, in many ways, passive, barely a participant in her own story. One can argue, as Renita Weems does, that in actuality, the story belongs to neither Hagar nor Sarah but to Abraham.

(They are important) only in so far as the role they play in being used by God to demonstrate the faithfulness of the divine promise to Abram: the promise that God would grant to Abram a legitimate heir who would, in turn, be a blessing to the nations. (Gn 12:1–3; 17:1–9)[7]

Hagar's story is, in many ways, one of surrogacy. She stood in for Sarai who, in her impatience and unfaithfulness, "lost sight of who she was in relation to the sovereign word of God, and in so doing, lost sight of reality itself."[8]

Sarai forgot who she was—a woman—and her role in the Jewish patriarchal tribal society—nobody. She lost sight of the reality that she and Hagar had more in common as women in that society that "that which divided them as Hebrew master and Egyptian slavewoman."[9]

Thus, both Hagar and Sarai can be considered victims—victims of a societal system which regarded men only and envisioned women only in terms of their relationship to those men—as daughter, wife, mother, or sister—unable to stand alone, with no identity they could claim for and of themselves.

As Weems notes:

At some time in all our lives, whether we are black or white, we are all Hagar's daughters. When our backs are up against a wall; when we feel abandoned, abused, betrayed, and banished; when we find ourselves in need of another woman's help; we, like Hagar, are in need of a woman who will "sister" us, not exploit us.[10]

The history of Black and white women's relations in this land, however, has too often been one of exploitation and the inability to recognize our shared commonalities and rejoice in our differences rather than shared "sisterhood." Thus, the story of the Egyptian slave, Hagar, and her Hebrew sister, Sarai, must also be seen as a story of "ethnic prejudices exacerbated by economic and sexual exploitation. Theirs is a story of conflict, women betraying women, mothers conspiring against mothers. Theirs is a story of social rivalry."[11]

Hagar was doubly, if not triply oppressed, suffering from the multiplicative oppressions of race, gender and class that continue to haunt African-American women today. Sarai was victim, yes, but also oppressor as well, unable or unwilling to recognize her own limited and prescribed status in Hagar and instead manipulating her husband, first, in order to be redeemed vicariously from her own barrenness and, secondly, in conspiring to have Hagar cast out into the desert with her child, once she, Sarai herself, had been able miraculously to bear a son of her own.

This odd psychological merging and disengaging has been constantly repeated throughout the history of Black and white women's relations in this country. It was often argued that the "physical assaults against black women in slavery; as well as the psychological deprivation resulting from their loss of control of their own persons" could be equated with the "White slave mistresses' psychological pain at their husbands' behavior."[12] Yet, as Linda Brent, herself a slave, wrote of her white mistress' actions:

> I was soon convinced that her emotions arose more from anger and wounded pride. She felt that her marriage vows were desecrated, her dignity insulted; but she had no compassion for the poor victims of her husband's perfidy. She pitied herself as a martyr; but she was incapable of feeling for the condition of shame and misery in which her unfortunate helpless slaves were placed.[13]

So they were cast out, out of sight and mind, of their sister-mistress so much so that, instead of even being allowed the maligned status of victim, Black women, historically, have been seen as perpetrators of the low status of both themselves and their entire people. A typical view stated by a white Southern woman in a newspaper in 1904 noted:

Negro women evidence more nearly the popular idea of total depravity then the men do....When a man's mother, wife and daughters are all immoral women, there is no room in his fallen nature for the aspiration of honor and virtue....I cannot imagine such a creation as a virtuous black woman.[14]

Yet, "still," in the words of Maya Angelou, "we rise."

Black women have borne many trials and tribulations in Western society. Yet there has always been that "something" that has enabled them to continue "to rise." Alice Walker credits Jean Toomer with articulating that unexpressed something that often the women themselves were unconscious of. She states:

When the poet Jean Toomer walked through the South in the early twenties, he discovered a curious thing: black women whose spirituality was so internal, so deep, so *unconscious*, that they were themselves unaware of the richness they held.[15]

She continues:

They dreamed dreams that no one knew—not even themselves, in any coherent fashion—and saw visions no one could understand.

They wandered or sat about the countryside moaning lullabies to ghosts, and drawing the mother of Christ in charcoal on courthouse walls.

They forced their minds to desert their bodies and their striving spirits sought to rise, like frail whirlwinds from the hard red clay.

Our mothers and grandmothers, some of them: moving to music not yet written. And they waited.

They waited for a day when the unknown thing that was in them would be made known; but guessed, somehow in their darkness, that on the day of their revelation, they would be long dead....

For these grandmothers and mothers of ours were not saints, but artists; driven to a numb and bleeding madness by the springs of creativity in them for which there was no release. They were creators, who lived lives of spiritual waste, because they were so rich in spirituality—which is the basis of art—that the strain of enduring their unused and unwanted talent drove them insane.[16]

They sought not merely a "room of one's own" in which to write, to be free, to create and be, in turn, re-created; they sought and were too often denied a life of their own, a being, a freedom which was of

11

their own making and owed nothing to the false largess of a master or mistress or, sometimes, even, of a husband. I think of Rebecca Jackson who, when called to serve as God's minister, despite the protestations of family, husband, and church [male] ministers, "left her husband and her brother's house...[to] become an itinerant minister who found fellowship (more accurately 'sistership') among other black women who organized 'praying bands'".[17] An illiterate woman, required to ask her brother to write letters for her, only to discover that he was putting his own words in, Jackson was "taught to read and write by the spirit within her."

> One day I was sitting finishing a dress in haste and in prayer. This word was spoken in my mind, "Who learned the first man on earth?" "Why, God." "He is unchangeable, and if He learned the first man to read, He can learn you." I laid down my dress, picked up my Bible, ran upstairs, opened it, and kneeled down with it pressed to my heart, prayed earnestly to Almighty God if it was consisting to His holy will, to learn me to read his holy word. And when I looked on the word, I began to read and when I found I was reading, I was frightened—then I could not read another word. I closed my eyes again in prayer and then opened my eyes,

began to read. So I done, until I read the whole chapter.[18]

How did they do it, we ask? How did they manage to keep their creativity alive year after year and century after century, when for most of the years Black people have been in America, it was a punishable crime for a Black person to read or write? And the freedom to paint, to sculpt, to expand their mind with actions of any kind simply did not exist.[19]

How did they do it; how did they continue to sing, to pray, to sew quilts worthy of hanging in exalted museums throughout this land? How did they do it—and, more importantly, how did they pass it on—to me and to my sisters, those before and those coming after me?

Walker tells us how:

> They were women then
> My mama's generation
> Husky of voice—stout of
> Step
> With fists as well as
> Hands
> How they battered down
> Doors
> And ironed
> Starched white
> Shirts

How they led
Armies
Headragged Generals
Across mined
Fields
Booby-trapped kitchens
To discover books
Desks
A place for us
How they knew what we
Must know
Without knowing a page
Of it
Themselves.[20]

And so our mothers and grandmothers have, more often than not anonymously, handed on the creative spark, the seed of the flower they themselves never hoped to see; or like a sealed letter they could not plainly read.[21]

They had the spirit within them—unnamed, perhaps sometimes but rarely unknown, the spirit which "brought them through" as they sang:

Sometimes I feel discouraged
And think my work's in vain
And then the Holy Spirit
Revives my soul again.

There is a balm in Gilead
To make the wounded whole
There is a balm in Gilead
To heal the sin-sick soul.

An anonymous Black ex-slave woman put it another way: "I have seen nothing nor heard nothing, but only felt the Spirit in my soul, and I believe that will save me when I come to die."[22] And so it did, not only after death but in the midst of life as well.

Where do we look for the source of that "creative spark" in our mothers and grandmothers, who sought to make flowers bloom wherever they found a barren piece of soil, whether of earthen clay or within a child's mind?

We who now are rooted in another soil, look homeward, to bell hooks, Africa, our mother land. As so many other creative Black women, realizes:

The spiritual world of my growing up was... very akin to those described in novels by Toni Morrison, Paule Marshall, or Ntozake Shange. There was in our daily life an ever present and deep engagement with the mystical dimensions of Christian faith. There was the secret love of the ancestors—the Africans and native Americans—who had given that new race of black folk, born here on this portion of earth, whole philosophies about how to be One with the universe and sustain life. That lore was shared by the oldest of the old, the secret believers, the ones who had kept the faith.

> ...in the traditional world of black folk experience, there was (and remains in some places and certainly in many hearts) a profound unspoken belief in the spiritual power of black people to transform our world and live with integrity and oneness despite oppressive social realities. In that world, black folks collectively believed in "higher powers," knew that forces stronger than the will and intellect of humankind shaped and determined our existence, the way we lived.[23]

It was that knowledge, formed within us as a part of our African heritage, passed down somehow from parent to child, which provided the fire that forged the strength which enabled us to not simply survive, but "move on up a little higher" each time. Although not a literate people at first, Black people, especially their women, were the "keepers of the faith," the "bearers of the culture" and the persistent "fanners of the flame" of that "creative spark" Alice Walker and others have come to recognize within us.

Gay Wilentz speaks in terms of "oralture," the oral stories and narratives, and oral literature, the writings that eventually emerged but which were still based on the oral histories handed down from generation to generation.[24] There is a "generational continuity" [the passing on of cultural values and personal history] which is traditionally the domain of women. This "generational continuity" can be seen to continue today as Black women writers focus "on Africa not only as historical ancestor, political ally, and basis for ideological stance but as part of a continuum in which Black women, before the slave trade and since, have recorded cultural history and values through their stories."[25] Black women writers such as Hurston, Walker, Morrison, Marshall, Bambara, as well as Cannon, Grant, Weems and many, many others immediately come to mind.

There exists also, Wilentz notes, a "cultural continuity" that exists in the perpetuation of African values and customs in the Americas.

> For African and African American writers, generational and cultural continuity—"to look back through our mothers"—is seen as a woman's domain. Oralture, and consequently, literature are part of many women's daily struggle to communicate, converse, and pass on values to their own and other children, and one another.[26]

In her comparative study of African and African-American women writers, Wilentz reveals and explores these continuities, especially how in African societies, many of which were matrifocal, "the cultural mores and value systems are passed down through the female members of the society, especially through and to the children."[27] Continuing this role, African-American communities have attempted (through their women) to retrieve and regather the often scattered and torn-apart roots of their African culture and reshape them in ways that are renewing and reviving in an African sense of being.

Although at times perhaps overstressed, it is important to note that there is a disparity between Western and pre-colonial African values and mores, especially regarding the "individual's responsibility to the community." A proverb often quoted notes that, "It takes an entire village to raise a single child."

Western culture, particularly in the twentieth century, has had a strongly capitalistic, individualistic approach to community structures: What is good for me will be good for the community. Thus, the heavy emphasis on the acquisition of national wealth. Historically, and even today in many African societies, there has been greater emphasis on the individual's accountability to the group....Another major disparity involves family structure. Many anthropological studies have looked at the nuclear versus the extended family—European/African, White/Black; in contrast to the nuclear family, the extended family is a way of branching out to a whole community through marriage. In this system, your responsibility is to all the children of the community, not merely your own. Coupled with consciousness of a continuum from the ancestors to the present generation and their descendants, this system creates a world view which, in many ways, conflicts with Western notions of family and society.[28]

Contrary to still popular beliefs which state that there was an irreparable breach between the people of Africa and their African-American descendants, what occurred in actuality was not the "spiritual holocaust" that some advocate but a reshaping and reforming notion of African spirituality in ways suitable to its new homeland. All connections between the African high god and lesser spirits, the ancestors, and the entire cosmos were not lost but were, consciously and unconsciously, reexamined under the new much harsher circumstances that the African peoples now found themselves in, but they were not destroyed and they did not become disheartened. As Dona Richard notes:

> ...Africa survived the middle passage, the slave experience and other trials in America because of the depth and strength of African

spirituality and humanism...[which] allowed
the survival of African-Americans as a dis-
tinctive cultural entity in New Europe....(It is
this) spirituality and vitality which defines
our responses to Western culture and that response is universally African.[29]

This African worldview that was transported
across the seas and survived amidst the chaos and
confusion of a new and dehumanizing way of life
enabled the slaves to make sense of their new sur-
roundings and their new life. It enabled them to
overcome deliberately imposed obstacles of separation from tribal and familial ties, loss of African
identity (supplanted by an imposed English name)
and lack of knowledge of the dominant language
to forge new life, new communities and new ways
of being in the world.

The African universe is conceived as a uni-
fied spiritual totality. The way of the world is
one in which all being is organically interrelated and interdependent. The essence of the
African cosmos is spiritual reality but one
not separate from the material, for both are
necessary for meaningful reality.[30]

The African philosopher John Mbiti acknowledges this:

Traditional religions are not primarily for the individual, but for his community of which he is part. Chapters of African religion are written everywhere in the life of the community, and in traditional society there are no irreligious people. To be human is to belong to the whole community, and to do so involves participating in the beliefs, ceremonies, rituals and festivals of that community. A person cannot detach himself from the religion of his group, his foundations, his context of security, his kinships and the entire group of those who make him aware of his existence.... to be without religion amounts to a self-excommunication from the entire life of the society, and African peoples do not know how to exist without religion.[31]

This self-understanding formed the core of the worldview of the men, women, and children brought to the United States in chains. It enabled then to bear up under the sudden and shattering catastrophe that had so irrevocably changed their lives and futures. Torn from natural kinship groupings and thrown among Africans with whom they had no tribal or language ties, they yet managed to build communities of love, caring, and fortitude that sustained and nurtured them in their struggle to survive the American holocaust—slavery.

Their ability to do this was a direct result of their African understanding and spirituality. Unlike the Western dualistic worldview that resulted in the separation of the sacred and the secular, affirming the one while damning the other, the African worldview is a holistic one wherein the human and the divine are conjoined. "The human is divine revealed in religious experience, and in the manifestation of the spirits in humanity," for example, in the African understanding of spirit possession. Albert Raboteau writes that the African gods were "carried in the memories of enslaved Africans across the Atlantic" and were revealed especially in the African-American (or Afro-Catholic) religions of Candomble, Santeria, and Vodoun.[32]

As I've discussed in a previous article on the African American experience of the Holy Spirit,[33] there was a "discontinuity...between the African heritage of spirit possession and the Black shouting tradition in the United States, yet, at the same time, a continuity can be seen in the context of the action, the patterns of motor behavior preceding and following the ecstatic experience." Both traditions involve "hand-clapping, foot-tapping, rhythmic preaching, antiphonal [call and response] singing and dancing."[34]

But a difference did exist, in how the spirit(s) was received and in how it behaved. The rituals were transformed from those in which the spirit actually invaded and "mounted" or "rode" the person to the loss of their own personality, to the experience of being "slain in the spirit" where one was filled with the love and goodness of the Holy Spirit while still retaining one's own sense of self. New rituals emerged, such as the "ring-shout," the "night songs," the "hush harbors," and the "prayer meetings" where one sang, prayed, and testified as one slave woman put it "to our soul's satisfaction"—a satisfaction that could not be achieved in the cold, stilted and artificial atmosphere of the enforced prayer meetings held by the slave masters on their plantations which slaves were required to attend and to "behave" at while having lessons on their inferiority yet "suitability" for slavery forced upon them.

It was in their own "invisible institution," the "hush harbors," that the slaves were free to create "vehicles for expressing the spirit and gaining strength" to persevere; it was there that the field hollers, worksongs, sorrow songs, spirituals and even the blues had their beginnings as the slaves rediscovered their own "sacred being through songs, ritual, music, and dance."[35] The experience was truly spiritual:

> As we laid down our burdens, we became lighter. As we testified and listened to others testify, we began to understand ourselves as

communal beings, no longer the kind of person that the slave system tried to make of us. Through our participation in these rituals, we become one. We become again, a community.[36]

Black women were very much involved in these activities; they were the singers, the pray-ers, the dancers, the testifiers, and, often, the preachers as well. We have heard the stories of Nat Turner, Denmark Vesey, Gabriel Prosser and others who, filled by the spirit, provoked rebellions in their midst, but rarely do we hear of the women who joined with them in the revolts, who nursed and healed the wounded, who taught them their letters as children in the first place, and who led their own quiet revolts, perhaps not as bloody, but just as demoralizing to their masters and mistresses who saw them only as docile, dull lackeys to be taught to do their own bidding. Rarely do we hear of the Ella Bakers, the Fannie Lou Hamers, the Rosa Parks, the Angela Davises, the Mary McLeod Bethunes, the Dorothy Heights, who fostered their own revolutions in our midst.

Bernice Johnson Reagon speaks in terms of "mothering"—a term not limited, however, just to those women who have actually given birth to children. For her, the understanding of a mothering generation encompasses "the way the entire community organizes daily to nurture itself and its future generations." She speaks of women who

> ...were the heads of their communities, the keepers of the tradition. The lives of these women were defined by their culture, the needs of their communities, and the people they served. Their lives are available to us today because they accepted the responsibility when the opportunity was offered—when they were chosen. There is the element of transformation in all of their work. Building communities within societies that enslaved Africans, they and their people had to exist in, at least, dual realities. These women, however, became central to evolving the structures for resolving areas of conflict and maintaining, sometimes creating, an identity that was independent of a society organized to exploit natural resources, people, and land.[37]

Mothering thus requires an ability and willingness to maintain traditions while reshaping them for future generations—discarding that which is not nurturing and upholding while incorporating that which is. Mothering reveals the many ways "a culture evolves and how and why changes occur in order to maintain the existence of a people."

Reagon affirms that

> within the story of the African diaspora,
> there is the opportunity to see a process of
> continuance and transformation at work
> among women cultural workers. Their strug-
> gle to contend with a new space entails defin-
> ing their people and children in new ways.
> That definition disrupted and threw into se-
> vere trauma cultural practices that had been
> nursed in African societies. Mothering, there-
> fore, required a kind of nourishing that would
> both provide food and stamina for survival
> within a cruel slave society and the passing on
> of traditions that would allow for the develop-
> ment of a community that was not only of but
> also beyond the slave society. These women
> had to take what they were given from their
> mothers and fathers (for as she notes, moth-
> ering is·not limited just to women) and make
> up a few things. Nurturing was not only rec-
> onciling what was passed down to them with
> day-to-day reality but also sifting and trans-
> forming this experience to feed this child, un-
> born, this new Afro-American community, in
> preparation for what it would face.[38]

It is this understanding or concept of "mothering" that is a critical aspect of womanist ways of
being in the United States today. It is by the con-

tinuous telling, despite the obstacles set in one's path, of "the history of one's people to future generations," thereby "imparting cultural values to the children of those generations, [that] Black women throughout the diaspora have kept their heritage [and as a result] the Black community alive and intact.[39]

These mothers, grandmothers, and co-mothers, aunts and play aunts, older sisters and god-mothers formed a community of women that renewed community and sustained the spirit in its midst.

The Black church has, historically, been the source of community life in all its variations—social, economic and cultural. Ironically, Black women, although the foundation of the church have not played significant leadership roles therein, although not for lack of trying. As Jacquelyn Grant asserted in 1979, Black women are indeed, the backbone of the church, but for too long the emphasis has been on "back" as in the background—out of sight—called forth only when needed—for Women's Day or other fund-raising events, to clean the church or to cook for and take care of the male ministers. The failure, Grant asserts, "of the Black Church and Black Theology to proclaim explicitly the liberation of Black women indicates that they cannot claim to be agents of divine liberation."

Fortunately, many Black women have taken to

heart Sojourner Truth's words, given at the 1852 National Women's Suffrage Convention:

> If the first woman God ever made was strong enough to turn the world upside down all alone; together women ought to be able to turn it rightside up again.[40]

Thus, "through the necessity of confronting and surviving racial (and sexual) oppression," oppressions joined in all too often by those who should have been their natural allies, Black men and white women, "Black women have assumed responsibilities atypical of those assigned to white women under Western patriarchy."[41]

Casting aside the myth of "True Womanhood," a myth they were never allowed to participate in fully, at any rate, Black women have forged new ways of being in the world which, in keeping with Alice Walker's terminology, they name as "womanist." They have done so because it was a necessary part of proclaiming who they were as women and as Black in a world and society which places little value on either status.

Christine Craig, in her poem, "The Chain," voices the contentious dialectic in which Black women find themselves:

> I no longer care, keeping close my silence
> has been a weight,

a lever pressing out my mind.
I want it told and said and printed down
the dry gullies,
circled through the muddy pools
outside my door.
I want it sung out high by thin-voiced elders
front-rowing murky churches.
I want it known by grey faces queuing under
greyer skies in countries waking
and sleeping with sleet and fog.
I want it known by hot faces pressed against
dust-streaked windows of country buses

   And you must know this now.
   I, me, I am a free black woman.
   My grandmothers and their mothers
   knew this and kept their silence
   to compost up their strength,
   kept it hidden
   and played the game of deference
   and agreement and pliant will.

It must be known now how that silent legacy
Nourished and infused such a line,
Such a close linked chain
to hold us until we could speak
until we could speak out
loud enough to hear ourselves
loud enough to hear ourselves
and believe our own words.[42]

And so today we continue to speak, out of our own contexts, from within our own lived experiences, confronting and challenging the silences which have kept us chained and bound to definitions of womanhood not of our own making, leaving us wounded, labeled as unfit mother, Jezebel, mammy. So we—in the footsteps of our sisters: Maria Stewart, Sojourner Truth, Ida B Wells-Barnett, Mary Terrell, Anna Julia Cooper, and so many others—declare that we, too, have something of value to say and that we *will* be heard.

Like Maria Stewart, ours is a God who directly intervenes in human affairs, "in the affairs of nations and individuals, against the wicked and on behalf of the downtrodden, but according to [God's] own timetable."[43] We are called to speak out as women by God as she herself was:

> The spirit of God come before me and I spoke before many...reflecting on what I had said, I felt ashamed....A something said within my heart, "press forward, I will be with thee." And my heart made this reply, "Lord, if thou will be with me, then I will speak for thee as long as I live."[44]

Her calling from God gave Maria the freedom to speak out and to act on the frontlines of Black moral and political leadership. But she also based her claim on women who, like herself, had received a similar call:

> What if I am a woman; is not the God of ancient times the God of these modern days? Did he not raise up Deborah, to be a mother, and a judge in Israel (Judges 4:4). Did not Queen Esther save the lives of the Jews? And Mary Magdalene first declare the resurrection of Christ from the dead?...St. Paul declared that it was a shame for a woman to speak in public,.... Did St. Paul but know of our wrongs and deprivations, I presume he would make no objections to our pleading in public for our rights.[45]

Black women are the "mothers," the bearers of African-American culture. They must speak for themselves because no one else is able or willing to speak for them nor are they willing any longer to be spoken for. They have gone back to their spiritual roots in Africa and the United States, recalling the spirits of those women of "stout step" and strong fists to discover, recover and reproclaim the African ethos which nurtured and sustained them from generation to generation down through the ages.

They have looked within themselves and their Black sisters to find that spirit of God which has always been with them but which, over the years of their sojourn in this strange land, they have, at times, lost contact with. They look to the writings of Black women, writings which affirm Black culture and Black community for their ways of seeing and of being are "alternative" rather than "oppositional":

> Much of African-American (male) literature has been oppositional, since the focus of the works tends to be on articulation of self as opposed to white men/white society. But the women may tell another story. Like their spiritual foremother Hurston, the African-American (female) writers demonstrate that documenting alternative cultural practices may open up other ways of seeing which have been lost both in opposition to and in competition by the dominant culture. One might say that the writings themselves are part of an alternative cultural practice, challenging the "canon" of African-American literature and criticism—and the practice is both residual and emergent. This alternative practice does not pose Afrocentric against Eurocentric binary oppositions; rather, it exposes some of the hidden modes of African-American community ties which have transformed both African retentions and Euro-American realities into a way of survival.[46]

This way of "mothering" is one in which womanists are also engaged recognizing that

> ...as long as the Black struggle refuses to recognize and deal with its sexism, the idea that women will receive justice from that struggle alone will never work....In the words of Sekou Touré: "If African women cannot possibly conduct their struggle in isolation from the struggle that our people wage for African liberation, African freedom, conversely, is not effective, unless it brings about the liberation of African women."[47]

Liberation cannot be partial or in stages. A womanist is one who is "committed to the survival and wholeness of an entire people, male *and* female. Not a separatist, except periodically, for health. Traditionally universalist...." This means that the struggle for liberation must be one that encompasses race, class and gender—at all levels, for all peoples. For, as Fannie Lou Hamer succinctly put it: "How can I hate another human being and expect to see God?"

Just as Katie Cannon proposes that "the Black women's literary tradition is the best available literary repository for understanding the ethical values Black women have created and cultivated in their participation in this society"[48] so, I would argue, does it serve as a source for discovering, uncovering and recovering the spiritual values and voice of Black women. In a religion (Christianity) and society (WASP) in which women's gifts as spiritual preachers, teachers and prophets were all too often disregarded and denied if not actively (and too often) violently opposed, the outlet for her dreams and visions, for the narrative of her encounters with the Holy (in whatever form that may take) were handed on in spiritual autobiographies, short stories, poems, and novels which were based, not on imagination, but very often on the lived experiences of the women writing them.

I want to share three such stories with you which show, as Cannon notes, the way in which "Black women writers authenticate, in an economy of expressions, how Black people creatively strain against the extended limits in their lives, how they affirm their humanity by inventing assumptions, and how they balance the continued struggle and interplay of paradoxes."[49] The first two narratives you are, I'm sure, familiar with: Celie's spiritual awakening in Alice Walker's, *The Color Purple*,[50] and Baby Suggs' "hush harbor" meeting in Toni Morrison's, *Beloved*;[51] the third, based on my own experience as a Black Catholic female theologian will not be as well known.

As we've come to know Celie, she is a passive, dispirited, abused woman—unable to stand up for herself because of the brutalizing life she has endured under, first, her stepfather, and then, her insensitive husband, Mister.

Yet, through the love of another woman, Celie is able not only to reframe her understanding of God but also to reclaim her own spirit and be a source of healing for all of those around her, thereby "mothering" a Black community, one which is viable economically, socially, and spiritually, into life.

Celie, in a conversation with Shug, admits that she no longer writes to God who she has always seen "as a man." One who "act just like all the other mens I know. Triflin', forgetful and lowdown." When Shug challenges her, she refuses to back down from her self-discovery and the empowerment it has brought her, despite a few qualms:

> All my life I never care what people thought about nothing I did. I say. But deep in my heart I care about God. What he going to think. And come to find out, he don't think. Just sit up there glorying in being deef, I reckon. But it ain't easy, trying to do without God. Even if you know he ain't there, trying to do without him is a strain.[52]

Shug then proceeds to share with Celie her own understanding of God, worked out from her own experience of rejection by her father, and overindulgence in men, money, wine and song.

> Here's the thing, say Shug. The thing I believe. God is inside you and inside everybody else. You come into the world with God. But only them that search for it inside find it. And sometimes it just manifest itself even if you are not looking, or don't know what you looking for. Trouble do it for most folks, I think. Sorrow, Lord.[53]

Celie, then, comes to a new, albeit still difficult, understanding.

> You have to get man off your eyeball, before you can see anything a'tall.
>
> Man corrupts everything, say Shug. He on your box of grits, in your head, and all over the radio. He try to make you think he everywhere. Soon as you think he everywhere, you think he God. But he aint. Whenever you trying to pray, and man plop himself on the other end of it, tell him to get lost, say Shug. Conjure up flowers, wind, water, a big rock.
>
> But this hard work, let me tell you. He been there so long, he don't want to budge. I hardly pray at all. Everytime I conjure up a rock, I throw it.[54]

And so she does, again and again, until she gets right with herself and the Spirit of God within her. And her healing, from incest and other forms of abuse, sexual and nonsexual, brings, as Toinette Eugene poignantly points out, a healing to all who come in contact with her, even Mister who is enabled by Celie's return to wholeness to find and reclaim his own.

Celie discovered her own spirituality and thus discovered her own voice, and used it to build a community. She represents that "thin line" of Black women who refused to keep silent. She and Shug had the gift of "drawing up the powers from the deep," a gift which Toni Cade Bambara noted in *Salteaters* is being lost to the "daughters of the yam." The silence of Black women which came into being, especially during the late 1960s, is a new silence as Michelle Wallace has realized:

> The black woman's silence is a new silence. She knows that. There has been from slavery until the Civil Rights Movement a thin but continuous line of black women who have prodded their sisters to self-improvement, to education, to an industrious and active position in the affairs of their communities. In their time a woman's interest in herself was not automatically interpreted as hostile to men and their progress, at least not by black people. Day by day these women, like most

women, devoted their energies to their husbands and children. When they found time, they worked on reforms in education, medicine, housing, and their communities, through their organizations and churches. Besides their other pursuits they took particular interest in the problems of their fellow beings, black women. Little did they know that one day their activities would be used as proof that black women had never known her place and has mightily battled the black man for his male prerogative as head of the household.[55]

They were known as "race" women, then, in the nineteenth and early twentieth centuries, or club women—women who sought the improvement of their race and of American society itself, women who fought against lynching, against the brutalization of Black men and women, women like Barnett, Cooper, Terrell, Elizabeth Lange and Henriette de Lille (founders of the first and second Black Catholic religious orders for women because the other orders would not accept them). Through the Christian church, despite opposition from black and white male preachers, and white women themselves, as I've already shown, these women "established an arena for discussion, debate, and implementation of their social, economic, and political agenda vis-à-vis white America

...fashioning the Bible as an "iconoclastic weapon"...and operating from a stance of "radical obedience," they compelled those who were not disposed to do so to listen to and take heed of their demands.

Toni Morrison reveals another one of these "God-touched" women to us in *Beloved*. For Baby Suggs, holy, also has the power of calling forth the Spirit, as her African mothers and grandmothers did, a gift we need to recover and reclaim now in the barren wasteland of the 1990's. She, too, was a "race" women who sought to heal, nurture, sustain and love her people.

Baby Suggs, holy, is a woman of God; one who left slavery and its destruction, which had left her with nothing but her great, strong heart. She is a woman called by God—as so many were then and now.

> Accepting no title of honor before her name, but allowing a small caress after it, she became an unchurched preacher, one who visited pulpits and opened her great heart to those who could use it.... Uncalled, unrobed, unanointed, she let her great heart beat in their presence. When warm weather came, Baby Suggs, holy, followed by every black man, woman and child who could make it through, took her great heart to the clearing.... In the heat of every Saturday after-

noon, she sat in the clearing while the people waited among the trees.[56]

And every Saturday afternoon, Baby Suggs, holy,
called forth the Spirit and sent it among the people causing them to laugh, dance, sing and cry—
and in response to their liberation by the
Spirit—she offered up "her great heart." And she
preached the gospel to them—not one of nega-
tion and fear; not one of self-hatred, denial or
pity but the gospel of love—love of self and love of
neighbor—but most importantly, love of their
beautiful, Black bodies.

She told them that the only grace they could
have was the grace they could imagine. That
if they could not see it, they would not have
it.

"Here," she said, "in this here place, we
flesh; flesh that weeps, laughs; flesh that
dances on bare feet in grass. Love it. Love it
hard. Yonder they do not love your flesh.
They despise it. They don't love your eyes;
they'd just as soon pick 'em out. No more do
they love the skin on your back. Yonder they
flay it. And O my people they do not love
your hands. Those they only use, tie, bind,
chop off and leave empty. Love your hands!
Love them. Raise them up and kiss them.
Touch others with them, pat them together,

stroke them on your face 'cause they don't
love that either. *You* got to love it, *you!* And
no, they ain't in love with your mouth.
Yonder, out there, they will not heed. What
you scream from it they do not hear. What
you put into it to nourish your body they will
snatch away and give you leavin's instead. No,
they don't love your mouth. *You* got to love it.
This is flesh I'm talking about here. Flesh that
needs to be loved. Feet that need to rest and
to dance; backs that need support; shoulders
that need arms, strong arms I'm telling you.
And O my people, out yonder, hear me, they
do not love your neck unnoosed and straight.
So love your neck; put a hand on it, grace it,
stroke it and hold it up. And all your inside
parts that they'd just as soon slop for hogs,
you got to love them. The dark, dark liver—
love it, love it, and the beat and beating heart,
love that too. More than eyes or feet. More
than lungs that have yet to draw free air. More
than your life-holding womb and your life-giv-
ing private parts, hear me now, love your
heart. For this is the prize." Saying no more,
she stood up then and danced with her twist-
ed hip the rest of what her heart had to say
while the others opened their mouths and
gave her the music. Long notes held until the

four-part harmony was perfect enough for their deeply loved flesh.[57]

We were a people then, a people of heart, and those hearts beat within us still, if we can only find the sounding notes that will cause them to beat in rhythm once again.

Baby Suggs, holy, was a woman and in her words, in her dance, in her calling forth of the children, the men and the women, to laugh, to dance, to cry, and ultimately, ultimately, to sing with every chord of their being, she personified what it means to be a womanist in the world today. For again, and it cannot be said often enough,a womanist is one who loves, who loves deeply, who loves strongly, who loves a community, a people, into being. And this is what we who call ourselves womanists must also do. For our world is "one where Black women teachers, preachers, and healers worked" and must continue to work "with as much skill, power and second sight" as we have available to us.[58]

I do not compare myself to either Celie or Baby Suggs except that we are all three Black women who love deeply and seek love in return, from and for our people and ourselves.

For most of my life, I have been an object—seeing myself only as I was reflected in the eyes of others. I was the odd one, "different" in some way, the one nobody knew quite what to do with. I was a

Black woman yet I did not fit the stereotypes which our society has placed upon Black women, ones which unfortunately my own culture has too often assimilated. I was always, in many ways, my own woman. I did not know my place. I simply persisted in quietly going my own way, never fully acknowledging the psychic costs, never sure where that way was leading me. In many ways, but without recognizing it, I was searching for myself, for my own identity, a step each child must take in order to grow into full maturity but one often denied Blacks, women and other so-called "minorities" in American society. I was hemmed in by stereotype, by prejudice, by misunderstanding, a misunderstanding sometimes wilful but often earnestly and painfully unconscious. I was fighting for my life, to be myself, to define myself, yet consciously aware that myself was different from other selves because of the racism and sexism embedded in our society today.

All too often in that struggle, my greatest challenge came from my own—Black men and women or white women—who distrusted my efforts and sought to impede my self-emancipation for reasons of their own. Thus, my struggle was two-sided. It involved the white world, that dominant structure which sought to label and thereby suppress my voice and my own world, that of African-Americans, who often saw me as a traitor to the race, as well as to Protestant Christianity, because I had dared to be different even though I had not been aware originally that I was being different. They, too, attempted to restrain and defeat me and silence my voice. Finally, after much prayer, discernment, and debate with God, I came to the realization that it was very important for my voice to be heard if only because so many were attempting to stifle it. I recognized that:

> Each time a woman begins to speak, a liberating process begins, one that is unavoidable and has powerful political implications...we see repeated the process of self-discovery, of affirmation in coming out of the closet, the search for a definition of our identity within the family and our community, the search for answers, for meaning in our personal struggles, and the commitment to a political struggle to end all forms of oppression.... When we write or speak...we establish our experiences as valid and real, we begin to analyze, and that analysis gives us the necessary perspective to place our lives in a context where we know what to do next.[59]

Today, I recognize that my words are heard in different ways by different people. They are heard in one way by those who seek to oppress and are seen as threatening and divisive; they are heard in another way by those engaged with me in the struggle for liberation of humanity, hopefully as affirming and liberating. I am a Black woman, for some, a symbol of nothingness, but for myself and many others, a sign of liberating faith.

It is the Black woman who "survived the long middle passage from Africa to America, bringing with her many of the diverse characteristics of her African mothers..., she gave her children love (and so today must we); cooked for them (as we must); protected them, told them about life, about freedom, about survival, about loving, about pain, about joy and about Africa."[60] And so must we continue to do so, for the children have lost touch with their past and are left searching, unguided and alone, for their futures.

> Our communities have become only "neighborhoods." The value images are gone. The teachers are gone. The counter-balancing forces are ineffective—there are no "elders," no priests, and so our children are suffering. They become enraged through disappointment at finding that what they have come from the spirit world to possess no longer exists. They turn on their parents, who have already abandoned them, and then they turn on themselves. Children of "hustlers" become "hustlers," and we are locked into despair.[61]

We are a spiritual people living in a profane society and we are in danger of losing, if we have not already done so, that spirituality which has consistently enabled us, with the help of Jesus the Christ, to "make a way out of no way." We have become like "ghosts," depersonalized and depersonalizing in constant search of "respect" and willing to kill or be killed for it. Yet, our children, ghosts who have no memory of a childhood, have no true idea of what respect truly means or how it can be honestly earned.

As Black women, we must reassert that spirituality and thereby regain the respect we once had for all our people but especially for the elders. We must do this not just for ourselves, not just for our Black men but for the sake of our children whose tears and cries call us out of ourselves to re-create that community of love we once had. As, historically, we have been the ones who were able to keep our families together and pass down the faith—a faith that was religious in more ways than usually understood in our individualistic and consumer-oriented society; a faith that encompassed all of life, making all of life sacred and therefore to be cherished; today we must rekindle that faith, blowing on the sparks that still linger deep within us, fanning them into a flame which will consume the world, not with bloodshed, not with wrath, but with love—a love that surpasses all other forms of love; an agape love. We must be the voices that speak when others fear to, recognizing with Audre Lorde:

> And when we speak we are afraid
> our words will not be heard
> nor welcomed
> but when we are silent
> we are still afraid
>
> So it is better to speak
> remembering
> we were never meant to survive.
>
> "Litany for Survival"

We were never meant to survive. So why then should we fear the obstacles set in our paths, the denial of our womanhood, the patronizing of our talents, the false limitations placed on us by those who cannot and never will understand who we are.

We are Black women—bearers of culture. We speak to and for "the formerly unvoiced members of [our] community—the wife, the barren woman, the young child, the mother, the grandmother."[62]

As Gay Wilentz asserts, Black women's existence is "a continuum, an invisible thread drawn through the women's stories to women readers and the men who will listen. Through their alternative mothering practice, these [Black women] writers construct residual herstory as emergent culture."[63]

We are the weavers of our future's tapestry; we and no others. And that tapestry is woven from the living and breathing souls of Black women, men and children in every walk of life, of every shade of skin from deep blue-black to palest peach-blushed tan. We are all Black in the fullest sense of the word. We are all children of Africa, the children of Hagar, the slave.

It is our task, if we are to follow in the footsteps of the strong and vibrant Black women whose lives I have so briefly shared with you in these pages, to rebuild our communities and the lives of the people therein, male and female.

It is our task to gather the scattered threads of our history, in this land and throughout the diaspora, joining with our sisters everywhere, and make it whole again, returning our past to ourselves, and thereby regaining the way to our futures for ourselves and posterity.

We are the teachers, acknowledging that: "If you educate a man, you educate an individual. If you educate a woman, you educate a nation."

This is not said to put down men but to raise up both women and men. It is time we climbed out of the dichotomous, dualistic trap in which we have been held for far too long to reclaim the understanding, which formerly never needed stating, that the enrichment of one does not require the impoverishment of another; the uplifting of one does not require the degradation of another; that in order to survive we must "walk together, children and not grow weary." We cannot live if half of our holistic selves have to be sacrificed so that the other might prosper—that is not a true or healthy prosperity—that is suicide.

It is time for Black women to reclaim their voices, voices somehow silenced in a "culture that depended on her heroism for its survival."[64] That voice has been silenced because women lacked the power, Mary Helen Washington believes, as the "disinherited" to recognize and claim their own power. Thus, the power of naming was left "in the hands of men—mostly white but some black...." As Washington relates: "Our ritual journeys; our 'articulate voices,' our symbolic spaces are rarely the same as men's...the appropriation by men of power to define tradition accounts for women's absence from our historical records."[65]

Shawn Copeland writes similarly when discussing how women scholars have appropriated the term "womanist," claiming, in so doing, "the power of definition, of self-definition, of self-naming."[66] Black womanist scholars, she states, "are struggling to define themselves and their experience—to be definers. For an African-American woman scholar to define herself, to name herself womanist is to embrace, to love her culture and re-ligio-cultural traditions, her people, her people's struggle, her own embodiment....For an African-American scholar to define herself, to name herself womanist is to tap the roots of the historically traditional liberation capability of Black women."[67]

Black women are making a claim, that they have the right and the responsibility in today's world to name their own experience, whatever it may be. Thus, the appropriation of Alice Walker's term "womanist" by Black women theologians is not only reasonable but responsible. Their doing so is not an effort to place on Walker's definition a burden it cannot bear, but to enlarge upon and deepen its meaning in a way that is uniquely theirs. It is an appropriation which sacralizes the term, bringing to bear the rich, dense, and diverse spiritual tradition that I have shared with you so briefly; a tradition which also goes beyond, opening itself to new and even more varied redefinitions, as Black women continue to claim their own identities as women who love and are loved in many, many different and glorious ways.

Katie Cannon effectively makes the point against those who would deny a spiritual and/or theological depth to the term "womanist":

By looking beyond and through historical "facts" for Black women's consciousness, womanist scholars undertake the systematic questioning and critical examination of the moral reasoning that enables Black women to refuse dehumanization and to resist the conditions that thwart life. A womanist liberation theo-ethical critique is a theoretical frame of reference that is at once a comparative and an ideal construct, asking new questions of the Black church community, in order to examine and confront openly the ideological nature and function of patriarchy in the Black Church.... A womanist liberation theological ethic...seeks...models that explore sacred power and benevolent cohumanity.[68]

She continues:

[Such an ethic] places Black women at the center of human social relations and ecclesial institutions. It critiques the images and paradigms that the Black Church uses to promote or exclude women...[serving] as a model for understanding the silences, limitations and possibilities of Black women's moral agency, by identifying Afro-Christian cultural patterns and forms, perspectives, doctrines, and values that are unique and peculiar to the Black Church community, in order to assess the dialectical tensions in Black women's past social relations as well as our current participation in the Black Church. A Black womanist liberation Christian ethic is a critique of all human domination in light of Black women's experience, a faith praxis that unmasks whatever threatens the well-being of the poorest women of color.[69]

Thus, a womanist way of being in the world is one which draws out the contradictions within the Black community and its most significant institution, the Black church, exposing them to the harsh light of a new day, and calling for constructive changes which are, in the truest sense, subversive as they shake the very foundations of the Black world, leading to a reappraisal and concomitant renewal of its relationship with and ties to the Black community and the white dominant society.

A womanist way of being in the world calls forth the Black experience of a personal God, one both transcendent as the bringer of justice and liberation and immanent as the one who walks and talks with us and tells us that we are God's own. It is a call for recognition of the power that is already within our grasp, as Ida B. Wells-Barnett recognized when speaking to a group of imprisoned Black men who expected only death:

Why don't you pray to live and ask to be freed...? Let all of your songs and prayers hereafter be songs of faith and hope that God will set you free.... Quit talking about dying, if you believe your God is all powerful, believe he is powerful enough to open these prison doors and say so.... Pray to live and believe you are going to get out.[70]

To be a womanist means to walk out on faith—not a blind faith that someone or something will somehow or other intervene on your behalf, but a blinding faith that reveals a God who batters down the gates of prisons where the righteous are held captive and sets them free, but only with their own participation in bringing about that freedom.

It is to be concerned not so much about the "hereafter" but more about the "here and now"—to feed the hungry but also teach them to feed themselves; to clothe the naked but also to set up schools where they will learn to make their own clothes; to open the eyes of the blind by providing educational resources and materials that enable them to learn of themselves and their past, better their present, and prepare for a better future of their own making; to set the captives free by breaking their minds open to a consciousness of themselves as a people who have survived and who will continue to survive, walking forward, unfettered, into a world of their own creation, if they believe not just in a "wonder-working" God but in themselves, God's creations, a people of power, creativity, intellect and hope.

To be a womanist is to be made whole—to be the continuation of the Black past and builders of the Black future. It encompasses the theological, yes, but also the political, cultural, social and economic traditions of Black being in the world. It is a way of keeping faith, of renewing that faith, and of passing on the faith of Black folk to the strong Black women and men who keep "a'comin' on."

To be a Black woman in today's world is to be an anomaly of sorts. It is, on the one hand, to be treated as someone who has performed miracles simply by continuing to persist in living life as she and she alone sees fit. On the other hand, it is to be narrowly watched, critiqued and judged for every action, every step, almost every breath taken. Black women today may no longer completely fit Zora Neale Hurston's often quoted words in *Their Eyes Were Watching God*[71]: "the nigger woman is the mule of the world," but neither has she been fully able to take her rightful place as a woman with creative and intellectual gifts to share with all the world in a liberated and liberating way.

Claiming and proclaiming one's voice as a Black woman, especially in today's Christian church, both Black and white, is an enterprise fraught with perils. But it is necessary, for we will only survive as a people, and thus as a nation if we acknowledge the gifts, not only of Black men and white women, but of Black women as well.

Bell hooks acknowledges the mixture of feelings that flow through us as we take those first often tentative steps:

> ...for women within oppressed groups who have contained so many feelings—despair, rage, anguish—who do not speak, as poet Audre Lorde writes, "For fear our words will not be heard or welcomed," coming to voice is an act of resistance. Speaking becomes both a way to engage in active self-transformation and a rite of passage where one moves from being object to being subject. Only as subjects can we speak. As objects, we remain voiceless—our beings defined and interpreted by others.[72]

The spirituality of Black women is a chain forged from many links, a tree with outstretched branches whose roots are buried deep in African soil and whose trunk and branches are flung far across the Atlantic Ocean, coming to rest in the nations of South America, the Caribbean, and North America. It is like the tree on Sethe's back—"A chokecherry tree. See, here's the trunk—it's red and split wide open, full of sap, and this here's the parting for the branches. You got a mighty lot of branches. Leaves, too, look like, and dern if these ain't blossoms. Tiny little cherry blossoms, just as white. Your back got a whole tree on it—in bloom. What God have in mind, I wonder."[73]

I wonder, too. The spirituality of Black women has been bathed in blood, nurtured by tears, held up and bound together by sweat. It is a living, growing thing which has spread forth across the world and throughout the nations, affecting everything that it touches.

What did God have in mind? Perhaps a witness, a witness to the cruelty and lust of the world but also of the endurance and perseverance that emerged from it—a people forged in pain and suffering who, yet, carried song and dance, prayer and exaltation of the Lord with them wherever they went.

Like Hagar, Black women have suffered. They have been seen as victims. As nothing and less than nothing yet paradoxically they have also been seen as super-women, as castrators of Black men, as both saint and devil. It is time to look at Hagar with renewed eyes—not as victim but as one who talked directly to God; one who, unlike Moses, or even Abraham, Toinette Eugene affirms, was admitted into God's very presence, for God heard the cries of Ishmael and was moved to respond.

Hagar is not a surrogate—one who suffers for humanity's sin. Rather she survived and her son grew to be a wild man who avenged the injustice done to his mother.

Black women are not surrogates either. The evil that has been done to us, in the names of God and man, are simply that—evil. Dolores Williams writes:

> God does not intend Black women's surrogacy experience. Neither can Christian faith affirm such an idea.... Jesus came for life, to show humans a perfect vision of ministerial relations that humans had very little knowledge of. As Christians, Black women cannot forget the cross, but neither can they glorify it. To do so is to glorify suffering and to render their exploitation sacred. To do so is to glorify the sin of defilement.[74]

God reaches out to Hagar in her abandonment and provides her with "new vision to see survival resources where she had seen none before." For Williams, "liberation in the Hagar stories is not given by God; it finds its source in human initiative." And as Hagar learned how to survive and acquire an "appropriate quality of life" for herself and her son, so also did the African slaves, accommodating "the Bible to the urgent necessities of their lives."[75] They recognized themselves in Hagar's experiences, Black women especially.

The African-American community has taken Hagar's story unto itself. Hagar has "spoken" to generation after generation of black women because her story has been validated as true by suffering black people. She and Ishmael together, as family, model many black American families in which a lone woman/mother struggles to hold the family together in spite of the poverty to which ruling class economics consign it. Hagar, like many black women, goes into the wide world to make a living for herself and her child, with only God by her side.[76]

And with God by her side, she, and therefore, the Black community is able to not only survive but to thrive.

The threat today is that the worldview of a conjoined cosmos, in which all of creation is intimately connected and interrelated, is being lost as Black American women and men fall victim to "American cultural values" which emphasize self over selflessness, personal possessions over communal wealth and individuality over community.

A return is required of us. We must return to our roots, reforge the links in our chain of continuity from Africa to the present, which have become rusty, worn and, in too many places, broken.

It is time, once again, to heed the voice of women, the mothers of us all. We must embark upon the path of much needed healing which will, in turn, free us to once more truly be ourselves as Black women and Black men.

We must heal the church, restoring it to its place as the source of community life but in a form that lifts up the gifts and talents of all—female and male, adult and child, married, single, divorced—rather than those of just a few. We must reshape our concepts of leadership into mutual forms that provide life for all. All of the barriers that have been artificially erected which cause separation and division must be removed and new relational ties (new but old in reality) that nurture, sustain, and heal must be put in their place.

We must return to the scripture that stated "the truth will set you free" and speak the truth to each other, talk to each other, share with each other, tell our stories and sing our songs once again and, in so doing, "name our pain, our suffering, and...seek healing."[77]

> Living a life with spirit, a life where our habits of being enable us to hear our inner voices, to comprehend reality with both our hearts and our minds, puts us in touch with divine essence. Practicing the art of loving is one way we sustain contact with our "higher self."[78]

Many of us have already seemingly lost the ability to love. It is that which must be retrieved, and womanists, whose way of being in the world is to love, one's self and others, regardless, can serve as catalysts for rekindling that love.

> In spiritual solidarity, Black women have the potential to be a community of faith that acts collectively to transform our world. When we heal the woundedness inside us, when we attend to the inner love-seeking love-starved child, we make ourselves ready to enter more fully into community. We can experience the totality of life because we have become fully life-affirming. Like our ancestors using our powers to the fullest, we share the secrets of healing and come to know sustained joy.[79]

It is our experience, not as victims, but as survivors, that is the foundation for the renewal of the Black community. Like Hagar, we have been harshly used in this world yet we have found strength in ourselves and in our faith in a God who fights on the side of the oppressed and we have continued to "move on up a little higher."

We are Hagar's daughters. We share in our sense of loss and abandonment yet we also share our knowledge of how to make it when times are difficult and the way is too dark to see. We have borne with us over the ocean the knowledge that enables us to continue to speak words of love, words of encouragement, words of empowerment. With Audre Lorde, we have learned "how to stand alone, unpopular and sometimes reviled, and how to make common cause with those outside the structures in order to define and seek a world in which we can all flourish."[80]

We are Black women, tall, strong, bending but rarely breaking. We stand as beacons of hope and also as bearers of culture. We are not superwoman; we cry, we hurt, we grow weary in the struggle; nor are we mankillers, for they are our fathers, our husbands, our brothers, and our sons. We cry out, with Fannie Lou Hamer: "I am sick and tired of being sick and tired." But having said that, we pick up our children, we shoulder our burdens, and we continue on. We seek love, a gentle hand, a loving heart, a sister-spirit to walk with through the storm.

> O, ye daughters of Africa! Awake! Arise! no longer sleep nor slumber, but distinguish yourselves, show forth to the world that ye are endowed with noble and exalted faculties.[81]

The daughters of Africa, Hagar's daughters, are awake and roam the earth, shaking it to its foundations, laboring to birth a new creation into healthy, healing and holy life.

NOTES

1. Mari Evans, "I Am A Black Woman," in Margaret Busby, ed., *Daughters of Africa* (New York: Pantheon Books, 1992), p. 300.
2. Diana L. Hayes, "To Be Black, Female, and Catholic," *New Theology Review,* 6, no. 2, May 1993, pp. 55–62, p. 57.
3. *Black Feminist Thought: Knowledge, Consciousness, and the Politics of Empowerment* (New York: Routledge, 1990), p. xii.
4. *Ibid.*, p. 11.
5. Maria W. Stewart, *America's First Black Woman Political Writer,* ed. Marilyn Richardson (Bloomington and Indianapolis: Indiana University Press, 1987), p. 21.
6. *Ibid.,* p. 30.
7. Renita J. Weems, *Just A Sister Away: A Womanist Vision of Women's Relationships in the Bible* (San Diego: Lura Media, 1988), p. 12.
8. *Ibid.*
9. *Ibid.*
10. *Ibid.,* p. 17.
11. *Ibid.,* p. 2.
12. Susan Thistlethwaite, *Sex, Race, and God: Chris-*

tian Feminism in Black and White (New York: The Crossroad Publishing Co., 1989), p. 33.

13. Bell hooks, *Ain't I A Woman?: Black Women and Feminism* (Boston: South End Press), p. 28.

14. *The Independent,* 56, March 17, 1904 as cited in Evelyn Brooks Higginbotham, *Righteous Discontent: The Women's Movement in the Black Baptist Church, 1880–1920,* p. 190.

15. Alice Walker, *In Search of Our Mothers' Gardens: Womanist Prose* (New York: Harcourt Brace Jovanovich, 1983), p. 231.

16. *Ibid.*

17. *Ibid.,* p. 76.

18. *Ibid.,* p. 74.

19. *Ibid.,* p. 234.

20. *Ibid.,* p. 242–43.

21. *Ibid.,* p. 240.

22. Clifton H. Johnson, ed., *God Struck Me Dead: Religious Conversion Experiences and Autobiographies of Ex-Slaves* (Philadelphia and Boston: Pilgrim Press, 1969), p. 172.

23. *Sisters of the Yam: Black Women and Self-Recovery* (Boston: South End Press, 1993), p. 8.

24. *Binding Cultures: Black Women Writers in Africa and the Diaspora* (Bloomington and Indianapolis: Indiana University Press, 1992), p. xii.

25. *Ibid.*

26. *Ibid.,* p. xiv.

27. *Ibid.*, pp. xv–xvi.
28. *Ibid.*, p. xviii.
29. "The Implications of African American Spirituality," in *African Culture: The Rhythms of Unity,* ed. Molefi Kete Asante and Kariamu Welsh Asante (Westport, Ct.: Greenwood Press, 1985), pp. 207–235; p. 207.
30. *Ibid.*, p. 210.
31. *African Religions and Philosophy* (Garden City, NJ: Doubleday Anchor Books), 1970, p. 3.
32. Diana L. Hayes, "Slain in the Spirit: Black Americans and the Holy Spirit," in *The Journal of the Interdenominational Theological Center,* XX, nos.1/2, Fall 1992/Spring 1993, pp. 97–115; p. 3.
33. *Ibid.*
34. *Ibid.*, p. 4.
35. Richards, p. 211.
36. *Ibid.*, p. 217.
37. Bernice Johnson Reagon, "Africa Diaspora Women: The Making of Cultural Workers," in *Women in Africa and the African Diaspora,* ed. by Rosalyn Terborg-Penn, Sharon Harley and Andrea Benton Rushing (Washington, D.C.: Howard University Press, 1987), pp. 167–180; p. 169.
38. *Ibid.*, p.177.
39. Wilentz, p. xxi.
40. Busby, p. xxxvii.

41. *Ibid.,* p. xxxxi.
42. in Busby, pp.555–56.
43. Stewart, p. 16.
44. *Ibid.,* p. 19.
45. *Ibid.,* p. 68.
46. Wilentz, pp. xxviii–xxviv.
47. Jacquelyn Grant, "Black Women and the Church," ed. by Gloria T. Hull, et al., *But Some of Us Are Brave: Black Women's Studies* (New York: Feminist Press, 1982), pp. 141–152; p. 147.
48. "Moral Wisdom in the Black Women's Literary Tradition," ed. by Judith Plaskow and Carol Christ, *Weaving the Visions: New Patterns in Feminist Spirituality* (San Francisco: Harper and Row, 1989), pp. 281–292; p. 285.
49. *Ibid.,* p. 285.
50. Alice Walker (New York: Pocket Books, 1982).
51. Toni Morrison (New York: Alfred A. Knopf, 1987).
52. *The Color Purple,* p. 200.
53. *Ibid.,* p. 202.
54. *Ibid.*, p. 204.
55. *Black Macho and the Myth of the Superwoman,* excerpted in *Feminism in Our Time,* Miriam Schneir, ed. (New York: Vintage Books, 1994), pp 295–96.
56. Morrison, p. 87.
57. *Ibid.,* pp. 88–89.

58. hooks, p. 9.

59. cited in Bell hooks, *Talking Back: Thinking Feminist, Thinking Black* (Boston: South End Press, 1989), p.12.

60. Wilentz, pp. 9–10.

61. Richards, p. 228.

62. Wilentz, p. xxxiii.

63. *Ibid.*

64. In Henry Louis Gates, ed., *Reading Black, Reading Feminist* (New York: Penguin, 1990), p. 5.

65. *Ibid.,* pp. 5–6.

66. "Roundtable Discussion: Christian Ethics and Theology in Womanist Perspective," *Journal of Feminist Studies in Religion*, 1989, p. 100.

67. *Ibid.*

68. *Ibid.,* p. 93

69. *Ibid.*

70. *Crusade for Justice,* ed. Alfreda Duster (Chicago: University of Chicago Press, 1970), p. 403.

71. Chicago: University of Illinois Press, 1978.

72. hooks, *Talking Back,* p. 12.

73. Morrison, p. 79.

74. *Sisters in the Wilderness* (Maryknoll, NY: Orbis Books, 1993), p. 167.

75. *Ibid.,* pp.4-5.

76. *Ibid.,* p. 33.

77. hooks, *Yam,* p. 16.

78. *Ibid.,* p. 185.
79. *Ibid.,* p. 190.
80. *Sister, Outsider: Essays and Speeches* (Freedom, Ca.: The Crossing Press, 1984), p. 112.
81. Stewart, p. 30.

The Madeleva Lecture in Spirituality

This series, sponsored by the Center for Spirituality, Saint Mary's College, Notre Dame, Indiana, honors annually the woman who as president of the college inaugurated its pioneering program in theology, Sister M. Madeleva, C.S.C.

1985
Monika K. Hellwig
Christian Women in a Troubled World

1986
Sandra M. Schneiders
Women and the Word

1987
Mary Collins
Women at Prayer

1988
Maria Harris
Women and Teaching

1989
Elizabeth Dreyer
Passionate Women: Two Medieval Mystics

1990
Joan Chittister
Job's Daughters

1991
Dolores R. Leckey
Women and Creativity

1992
Lisa Sowle Cahill
Women and Sexuality

1993
Elizabeth A. Johnson
Women, Earth and Creator Spirit

1994
Gail Porter Mandell
Madeleva: One Woman's Life